GRAPHIC BIOGRAPHIES

MATTHEW HENSON
Arctic Adventurer

by B. A. Hoena
illustrated by
Phil Miller and Charles Barnett III

Consultant:
Genevieve LeMoine
Curator/Registrar
The Peary-MacMillan Arctic Museum
Brunswick, Maine

Capstone press

Mankato, Minnesota

Graphic Library is published by Capstone Press,
151 Good Counsel Drive, P.O. Box 669, Mankato, Minnesota 56002.
www.capstonepress.com

1 2 3 4 5 6 10 09 08 07 06 05

Library of Congress Cataloging-in-Publication Data
Hoena, B. A.
    Matthew Henson : Arctic adventurer / by B.A. Hoena ; illustrated by Phil Miller and
Charles Barnett III.
        p. cm.—(Graphic library. Graphic biographies)
    Includes bibliographical references and index.
    ISBN 0-7368-4634-4 (hardcover)
    1. Henson, Matthew Alexander, 1866–1955—Juvenile literature. 2. African-American
explorers—Biography—Juvenile literature. 3. North Pole—Discovery and exploration—Juvenile
literature. I. Miller, Phil, ill. II. Barnett, Charles, III, ill. III. Title. IV. Series.
G635.H4H642 2006
910'.92—dc22   2005005774

Summary: In graphic novel format, tells the life story of explorer Matthew Henson and his
expedition to the North Pole with Robert Peary.

Art Director
Jason Knudson

Designer
Bob Lentz

Colorist
Scott Thoms

Editor
Tom Adamson

Editor's note: Direct quotations from primary sources are indicated by a yellow background.

Direct quotations appear on the following pages:
Pages 4, 5, 6, 8, 10, 11, 14, 20 (Henson's line), 22, 25, 26, from *Dark Companion* by Bradley
    Robinson (New York, R. M. McBride, 1948).
Page 13, from *The North Pole* by Robert E. Peary (New York: Cooper Square Press, 2001).
Pages 16, 17, from *North Pole Legacy* by S. Allen Counter (Amherst: University of Massachusetts
    Press, 1991).
Page 20 (Peary's line), from "Matthew Henson" by Donald D. MacMillan (*The Explorers Journal*
    Fall 1955).

TABLE OF CONTENTS

In 1883, Captain Childs died.

I've been at sea for five years. Without Captain Childs, it's time to move on.

Now 17, Henson searched for a new job. He soon learned that his experiences and skills wouldn't help him find a good job. He was hired only for difficult, low-paying jobs.

Henson loaded heavy crates onto ships in Boston, Massachusetts.

In Providence, Rhode Island, he worked as a bellhop at a hotel.

He had a backbreaking job digging ditches in Buffalo, New York.

Peary's Dream

In 1888, Henson and Peary returned to the United States. Peary worked at the League Island Navy Yard in Philadelphia, Pennsylvania. He got Henson a job there as a messenger.

One day, Peary called Henson into his office.

I'm going to explore the Arctic. I'd like you to come along.

But what is there for me to do? I'm not a scientist.

Build sledges, hunt, drive a dog team, make cook stoves, sledge supplies through torrents of ice and snow.

Sounds like a great adventure!

Shortly after their arrival, an Inuit family visited Peary's camp. Everyone was surprised at the Inuit's reaction to Henson.

The Inuit thought Henson was a lost member of their people because of his dark skin.

During this trip, the Inuit taught Henson and Peary important skills. The Inuit taught them how to build igloos, how to hunt musk ox and polar bear, and how to drive a sledge.

Peary had a ship, the *Roosevelt*, built for his Arctic trips. The ship's powerful engines and sturdy hull allowed it to cut through icy waters.

In 1908, Henson, age 42, left with Peary for another try to reach the North Pole. They stopped at the Inuit village of Etah, Greenland. They traded for furs and sled dogs. They also hired Inuit to help them on their trip.

Mahri Pahluk!

Hi-nay-nuk-who-nay?

I'm doing well, my friends.

The Inuit called Henson *Mahri Pahluk*, which meant Matthew the Kind One or Big Matthew.

KRRREEEEKK

The *Roosevelt* fought its way past huge icebergs and through icy waterways. In September, it reached Ellesmere Island, off the northwestern coast of Greenland. There, it became locked in ice.

Huk! Huk!

Henson began sledging supplies to Cape Columbia, the northern-most point of Ellesmere Island. The group set up a camp of igloos there and called it Crane City. Arctic winters have little daylight. Peary's party didn't want to travel in darkness all the time, so they waited at Crane City until spring.

During winter's long, dark hours, Henson built sledges and prepared supplies. Ootah helped Henson hunt musk ox.

O-ming-mak.

I see him, Ootah.

Other times, the ice broke apart as it shifted, causing leads. Peary named one stretch of open water the Big Lead.

It's like a half-mile wide river, Matt! There's no way around it.

We'll have to wait until the temperature drops and ice forms.

The Big Lead scared the Inuit. They thought it was caused by a devil named *Tahnusuk* who wanted to swallow them in ice.

Seegloo, don't be afraid.

Peary works for a devil more powerful than Tahnusuk. It's called the U.S. Navy.

After a six-day wait, the ice finally froze thick enough for them to cross.

19

After one month, Henson and Peary were about 150 miles from the North Pole.

Well, Bartlett, here's where your team goes back.

Henson must go all the way. I can't make it without him.

Don't worry, captain, we'll make it.

Only Henson and four Inuit continued to the North Pole with Peary.

After Bartlett headed back, Henson was in charge of the lead group. He, Ootah, and Seegloo used pickaxes to make a trail over the rough ice.

The next day, Peary took out his navigational equipment. By measuring where the sun was in the sky, he could determine how far north they were.

The North Pole at last!

The North Pole! We are the first to stand here!

Peary took a picture of Henson and the four Inuit standing at the North Pole.

After reaching their goal, Henson, Peary, and the Inuit still had a hard journey home. They celebrated by resting for a day. Then they headed back to Cape Columbia, reaching land two weeks later.

GREENLAND

ETAH

ELLESMERE ISLAND

CRANE CITY/ CAPE COLUMBIA

ARCTIC OCEAN

NORTH POLE

Peary's "Colored Assistant"

After returning to the United States, Peary received many awards.

Henson received little recognition.

For the discovery of the North Pole, the National Geographic Society awards you this gold medal.

NATIONAL GEOGRAPH

GREENLAND

Who's that standing behind Peary?

It's his colored assistant.

During the years following his trip to the North Pole, Henson struggled to find a good job. He wrote to Peary several times. But Peary did not help him. Their worlds were once again divided into white and black.

In 1913, Henson found work parking cars in Brooklyn, New York. One day, politician Charles Anderson saw him.

This is no job for you. Look what you've accomplished.

I'm a Negro. Whatever I did with Peary makes no difference.

Henson, our country owes you something!

Anderson and other African American leaders helped get Henson a government job. In 1913, Henson became a clerk for the U.S. Customs Bureau in New York City. He worked there until his retirement in 1937.

Matthew Henson's life was filled with hardships. At an early age, he lost his parents. He was judged by the color of his skin instead of by his abilities. And even after braving the dangers of the Arctic, few people recognized him for his accomplishments.

MATTHEW ALEXANDER HENSON
CO-DISCOVERER OF THE NORTH POLE

On March 9, 1955, Henson died at age 88. He was buried in a small cemetery in Maryland.

About 30 years after his death, Henson's body was moved to Arlington National Cemetery. Many American heroes, including Peary, are buried there. Today, Henson receives equal recognition. He is considered the co-discoverer of the North Pole.

MATTHEW HENSON

* Matthew Alexander Henson was born August 8, 1866, near Nanjemoy, Maryland. Henson had two sisters and three brothers.

* People aren't sure when Henson's parents died. Good records were not kept for African Americans in the 1800s. But Henson's parents died when he was very young. He was on his own by age 12.

* In 1893, Henson adopted an Inuit boy, Kudlooktoo, whose mother had died. He helped take care of Kudlooktoo during his visits to the Arctic. After the 1909 North Pole expedition, Henson lost touch with him.

* After the 1893–1895 trip, Henson wasn't sure he wanted to go back to the Arctic. An African American friend, George Gardner, told Henson that he had to go back to prove that African Americans could play an important role in history-making events.

* In 1906, Henson had a son, Anaukaq, with an Inuit woman, Akatingwah. Henson never saw them after he left the Arctic in 1909. In 1986, Anaukaq and his sons traveled to the United States to meet some of Henson's relatives.

Henson died March 9, 1955, at age 88.

 In 2000, 91 years after the discovery of the North Pole, the National Geographic Society awarded Henson the Hubbard Medal. The organization had given the same award to Peary in 1906.

 ## INUIT GLOSSARY:

- **Hi-nay-nuk-who-nay?**—Hello, how are you?
- **Huk! Huk!**—the command to get sled dogs moving
- **Inuit**—the people
- **Mahri Pahluk**—Matthew the Kind One or Big Matthew
- **O-ming-mak**—musk ox

GLOSSARY

igloo (IG-loo)—the traditional house of the Inuit, made of sod, wood, stone, blocks of ice, or hard snow

Inuit (IN-yoo-it)—native people of the Arctic

lead (LEED)—area of open water on a frozen body of water

porter (POR-tur)—someone who carries luggage for people at a railroad station or hotel

pressure ridge (PRESH-ur RIJ)—tall piles of ice formed by large sheets of ice on the Arctic Ocean that smash together

racism (RAY-sih-zuhm)—the belief that one race is better than another race

sledge (SLEJ)—to drive a dog team; or the sled that is used by a dog team.

torrents (TOR-uhnts)—huge outpourings of something

valet (va-LAY)—a person who attends to the personal needs of another person

INTERNET SITES

FactHound offers a safe, fun way to find Internet sites related to this book. All of the sites on FactHound have been researched by our staff.

Here's how:

1. *Visit www.facthound.com*
2. Type in this special code **0736846344** for age-appropriate sites. Or enter a search word related to this book for a more general search.
3. Click on the **Fetch It** button.

FactHound will fetch the best sites for you!

READ MORE

Armentrout, David, and Patricia Armentrout. *Matthew Henson.* Discover the Life of an American Legend. Vero Beach, Fla.: Rourke, 2004.

Currie, Stephen. *Polar Explorers.* History Makers. San Diego: Lucent, 2002.

Gaines, Ann. *Matthew Henson and the North Pole Expedition.* Journey to Freedom. Chanhassen, Minn: Child's World, 2001.

Litwin, Laura Baskes. *Matthew Henson: Co-discoverer of the North Pole.* African-American Biographies. Berkeley Heights, N.J.: Enslow, 2001.

Weidt, Maryann N. *Matthew Henson.* History Maker Bios. Minneapolis: Lerner, 2003.

BIBLIOGRAPHY

Counter, S. Allen. *North Pole Legacy: Black, White, and Eskimo.* Amherst: University of Massachusetts Press, 1991.

Henson, Matthew. *A Negro Explorer at the North Pole.* Montpelier, Vt.: Invisible Cities Press, 2001.

Peary, Robert E. *The North Pole.* New York: Cooper Square Press, 2001.

Robinson, Bradley. *Dark Companion.* New York: R. M. McBride, 1948.

INDEX